AMAZON'S FBA

STEP-BY-STEP GUIDE TO LAUNCHING YOUR PRIVATE LABEL BUSINESS AND MAKING MONEY ON AMAZON

BY: GREG ADDISON

© **Copyright 2016 - All rights reserved.**

In no way is it legal to reproduce, duplicate, or transmit any part of this document in either electronic means or in printed format. Recording of this publication is strictly prohibited and any storage of this document is not allowed unless with written permission from the publisher. All rights reserved.

The information provided herein is stated to be truthful and consistent, in that any liability, in terms of inattention or otherwise, by any usage or abuse of any policies, processes, or directions contained within is the solitary and utter responsibility of the recipient reader. Under no circumstances will any legal responsibility or blame be held against the publisher for any reparation, damages, or monetary loss due to the information herein, either directly or indirectly.

Respective authors own all copyrights not held by the publisher.

Legal Notice:

This book is copyright protected. This is only for personal use. You cannot amend, distribute, sell, use, quote or paraphrase any part or the content within this book without the consent of the author or copyright owner. Legal action will be pursued if this is breached.

Disclaimer Notice:

Please note the information contained within this document is for educational and entertainment purposes only. Every attempt has been made to provide accurate, up to date and reliable complete information. No warranties of any kind are expressed or implied. Readers acknowledge that the author is not engaging in the rendering of legal, financial, medical or professional advice.

By reading this document, the reader agrees that under no circumstances are we responsible for any losses, direct or indirect, which are incurred as a result of the use of information contained within this document, including, but not limited to, —errors, omissions, or inaccuracies.

TABLE OF CONTENTS

Introduction 7
Chapter One What Is Fulfillment By Amazon? 9
Chapter Two Benefits Of The Model 15
Chapter Three Setting Yourself Up 21
Chapter Four Some Products Are Better Than Others 27
Chapter Five Some Suppliers Are Better Than Others 33
Chapter Six To Continue or to Exit 43
Chapter Seven Marketing and Promoting the Product 55
Chapter Eight Getting Reviews 91
Conclusion 107

INTRODUCTION

The world is changing. It always has been, though now the ENTIRE world can change together. Globalization has connected people everywhere. The medium? The Internet. It would not be an overstatement to consider the proliferation of the Internet a revolution. It has the power to transform the entire planet and do it in real time. The globalization of the economy, partially fueled by the Internet, is also a major step forward for humanity. A Pakistani can contract with a Brazilian to sell merchandise manufactured in Thailand to people living in Canada. Human relations are more important than ever as humanity talks to each other. Why would they want their nations to fight? That means less money for them all (unless they're selling military equipment, but that's a special case and usually closely guarded secrets, anyway).

The Internet has opened a huge avenue of capitalism and created highly diverse jobs and even business models. One major way for old brick-and-mortar retailers to cut costs is to develop a website – few employees, no physical location for customers, little costs in the way of training, often very low taxes. It also allows businesses to react instantly to changing market conditions by updating their websites. If a competitor is offering a sale, an online store can immediately counteroffer, and all customers will know. That is not possible for brick-and-mortar stores, except for the customers already in the single building. The Internet, however, does not care whether you are a massive corporation with 5,000 stores across the country or a small town artesian making rare trinkets by hand from locally sourced from Wisconsin tea leaves. Both are viable if the customers are there. And the internet is probably the only viable option for the latter.

Aside from the great security at large for humanity and business, there is also something good in it for you, specifically. Whether you grew up with the Internet or you know a time before, this business revolution is wide open for opportunists to make some money. Whether you sell literal cargo ships of merchandise or if you just sell a little, there is a technique you can use to reduce costs and headaches. This involves a once-small company known as Amazon.

Amazon's Fulfillment by Amazon is a way for you to take advantage of the expertise from a behemoth of a company. As we will see, they handle many aspects of logistics so you can focus on the marketing or manufacture of your products. Let's find out how you, too, can leverage one of the world's largest companies' knowledge to increase your own profits.

CHAPTER ONE

WHAT IS FULFILLMENT BY AMAZON?

Many of you may have heard of Amazon FBA. The main strategy here is to use Amazon and its vast reserve of resources and knowledge to help you do logistics for your company. You will need to come up with a product, market it, entice the customers, direct the customers, deal with customer service (to a degree), manage your own cash flows and financials, and really do most of the business. However, Amazon is, first and foremost, a logistics company. Amazon has bought warehouses in strategic locations in order to cut shipping times while still balancing cost (a warehouse in Manhattan would indeed ship fast but cost more than a skyscraper). They have also invested heavily in research for optimizing how to store all that stuff they sell. The process is becoming more and more automated, and someone has to invest the money into the research to build these robotic staffs.

You, however, are not that someone. Similar to how Amazon has bought huge server farms and rented out space from them, they also do it with their warehouse space. The main idea is you send your product to Amazon, and they will do pretty much everything else dealing with logistics. You get to leverage the space and research of Amazon in return for a fee you pay them.

Amazon knows how to run multiple businesses at a time as they have the experience of working with people from around the world. They are able to handle the large problems of the business so that you are able to focus more on what needs to be done on your side. They have the space to provide the storage for your product, and they have the experience to know how to handle maintaining the service. All you would need to do is focus on the website and sending your products to Amazon. They will be able to handle the rest through their own area of the logistics and supply chain management. Here, it is all about providing the right amount of storage space for each product.

Logistics and supply chain management are no easy feats. There is even a whole branch of research into the area at companies and even at universities. While you will need to get your supplier, you will not have to worry about finding a location for your warehouse and staffing it. Furthermore, you can let Amazon handle a large portion of the customer service. This does not mean you won't have to do work for your business. It is still your business. You will still need to be in contact with your customers and your suppliers, but Amazon will take the burden of first-line customer service – if you prefer.

With this system, it becomes easier to run a business and selling your own products from the comfort of your own home. Normally, you as the manager would have to worry about the shipping, product storage, and customer basics such as reviews. But with this system of management in Amazon, it is easier to find what you need for the business, and they are willing to help you along the way as you create the product for yourself.

Why does Amazon do this? Aside from the possible promotion of entrepreneurial spirit, Amazon has invested a lot of money and has great locations. They realize they can make even more money by using some of that space and some of their connections (with certain shipping firms). You are also required to sign up for an Amazon Seller account, which generally charges fees. There are also incentives to list your products directly on the website instead of other avenues, which drives traffic to their website. As you bring more business for yourself, you invariably bring more business for Amazon because they can advertise and cross-sell directly from your listing.

It is important to realize just how large the name Amazon is. People may even remember how small the company used to be and how it has grown to be all over the world. Recognized by many different large corporations that work together through the management of Amazon for their products. When you agree to be a part of this business connection with Amazon, you are making a deal with them. A deal where they will get advertising as more people see or buy your product. This way, you get your product sold as they increase their name benefits. Because they want more people headed over to their website, they will make it easier for the business owners to follow through this process. Whether you are an individual that is just starting their own business, or you are part of a company that has existed for decades, they work to make it easier for you so they can benefit as well.

The process within Amazon is, as is most processes with the company, relatively easy to move through. It can be done by anyone, and even if you have never worked with an online store before, you will be able to pick it up quickly. Certain types of products may not be as suited to the deal as others. Amazon says they should be "e-commerce ready," which means they are easy to ship and can withstand such an ordeal. If you are selling live cats, this is not for you. You cannot ship such things. However, if you are selling cat dolls, then this is for you. Or cat toys. Or cat pictures. Anything that one would generally consider factory-producible merchandise can benefit from Amazon FBA.

One thing to note is that if you are not selling a large quantity, it may be better to go your own route. Amazon will happily accept your business and work with you, but if you can only produce a single one-of-a-kind armchair once every three months, it is not worth storing them at Amazon. If you have highly customized work, this also may not be the best place for you to hawk your wares. Unique or customized works require more involvement between the customer and the producer, and because you are not moving large quantities, you do not have as much of an incentive to utilize a large logistics system.

CHAPTER TWO

BENEFITS OF THE MODEL

While Amazon certainly gains a lot from this aspect of their business, you also reap the profits. There are numerous benefits to using Amazon FBA, which includes some of the features that may seem exclusively held to Amazon only. Amazon outlines some of the benefits on their website, but there are numerous others.

First, you get Amazon's name attached to your business. This may not seem like it means a lot, but the trust Amazon has built with its customers is all encompassed in its name. If you are running your own website, you need to build that trust first. In an age when there are so many fraudulent websites and scams, it can be hard to get that trust. But if you use Amazon as the logistics manager, you customers will know that the product actually exists, and they won't be throwing money into the unknown. Or worse, have their personal information stolen.

Furthermore, Amazon will handle the customer service and returns. They state that they handle all of this for items purchased from Amazon. That now includes your merchandise.

And with a seller account, you can sell in Canada and Mexico. Don't speak Spanish or French? How will your customers from Quebec or Mexico interact with you? Should you just forget about them? You won't have to worry about that if Amazon takes care of it for you. You won't have to worry about dealing with returns and re-shelving your product, either, as Amazon will do that for you as well. Just make sure to check their Returns Processing Fees, because certain items will cost you a bit more to return to your inventory. Amazon also has a very convenient, easy to understand, and well-programmed returns area of their website where your customers can do everything electronically. You won't have to waste time dealing with clients who just want to return something because of a defect; instead, you could be out getting new customers.

That customer service is not only limited to a few hours a week, either. You may need to sleep, but Amazon does not. An alternative for you is to hire a sales and customer service team, but that costs more money, and you are trying to keep your costs as low as possible. Amazon will answer those customer service inquiries 24 hours a day, 7 days a week, 365 days a year. There is no day that Amazon is off and cannot take your customers' calls. Remember, you still need to talk to your customers, but for the simple stuff, you won't need to hire extra staff or become some kind of robot.

Another major advantage to using Amazon for your fulfillment is the free shipping associated with the Prime Accounts. Many people buy things online often and do not like to pay extra shipping charges for every single item the purchase. If you are shipping things yourself, you will either need to factor the cost of shipping into your business or pass it on to your customers. No one wants to find a great gift then realize they have to pay another 15% just to get it to their door. That is a big driver behind Amazon Prime accounts: free shipping. Since your merchandise will be stored in an Amazon warehouse and shipped using Amazon's partner carriers, you will reap the benefit of that business structure. Prime Members on Amazon can get your product shipped to them for free. People love to hear something is free, even if it only saves them a little bit of their money. Moreover, for those who do not have Prime accounts, there is still the possibility that your product will ship to them for free. Under the Small and Light program, you will be able to ship certain products (presumably they are small in size and light in weight) for free to all customers. Usually, these are your high-turnover products that sell quickly and are not that expensive. These are often packaged in with other, more bulky orders, to optimize the volume of a box. They ship for free because the carriers do not charge much more for the negligible weight and no size increase (they are packed into every nook and cranny of the already measured box for the bigger thing).

That shipped merchandise gets to the customer faster, too. Fulfillment by Merchant products, sold on Amazon, still needs to be picked and packed by the merchant (that would be you). Amazon is more likely better than you at doing this, and they are certainly better than some merchants. This means that you can get your products to your customers faster than companies who try to do it themselves. Furthermore, when Amazon finally develops their 2-hour delivery system by drone, do you expect to be able to beat that? Most companies do not. Certainly, Amazon will reserve drone service for their own products for some time, but it will likely come to pass eventually that FBA customers will also be able to ship by drone. By that time, it may not be as novel to do so, but certainly, it will look cooler for your product to be shipping to your customer in a couple of hours by a flying robot than your competitor who takes five days to send the same thing in the regular, boring snail mail.

Another major advantage that is often overlooked is data security. Unless you are employing a development team for your website, your store may not be secure. Your customers do not want to receive an email that their credit card information has been stolen as a direct result of your website being hacked. However, if you list on Amazon, the payments can go through their website. It should be no surprise that a huge corporation like Amazon has a lot of money invested in internet security and will always be vigilant about it. Even if you use another service for your payments on your website, you can add Amazon as another avenue.

Since you need an account and can sell on their website, does this mean you should shut down your own website? Absolutely not! While Amazon has a great reputation and a lot of resources for you, you may already have an established website that your customers know and prefer. That is no problem whatsoever because another advantage to FBA is that you can still fulfill orders from other channels. Keep in mind that Amazon cannot cross-sell on their website if you do not list it there, so there are slightly higher fees associated with fulfillment through a channel that is not Amazon.com. However, if you have a well-established website, you have two choices.

First, you can redirect all your traffic to your listings on Amazon.com and effectively turn your site into a marketing platform, while the actual sales platform is Amazon. Amazon makes migrating quite simple, and you can even list your items in bulk to avoid dealing with a large number of listing. Even if you have a fully developed inventory management system, you can integrate it with Amazon's API. Conversely, if you already have a large website and would be linking away from your site too often, migration is not the only option. You can continue to sell everything from your site and handle all the payments through your payment processor of choice. You just need to let Amazon know when you to ship. This is considered going through a non-Amazon channel, and, as stated, involves a higher fee.

Conversely, if you can't program or don't want to deal with SEO to get yourself to the first page on search engines, you can easily set yourself up Amazon only. You don't have to worry about security (as mentioned), but you also don't have to worry about programming, servers, your site crashing, overloaded payment systems (unless you have some kind of amazing product you won't crash Amazon). This is great for entrepreneurs who are looking just to get into the game. It cuts technology costs, in knowledge, time, and money, to nothing. That is good news for anyone who wants to work on marketing and finding customers – or, in other words, building the business itself.

CHAPTER THREE

SETTING YOURSELF UP

The process of getting set up on FBA itself is not that difficult. You simply sign up for a Seller Account on Amazon, and you can start. After you have your account, you will need to enter your product listings (assuming you will be using Amazon's platform for your sales). If you already have a large inventory system, you will benefit from the use of the Amazon API. A word of caution to those who are starting out or not: make sure you have a system in place for inventory management. If you are used to going to the back storeroom to check on inventory and doing it once a month, you won't be able to do that anymore. Your product will be at the Amazon warehouses, and you won't be able to physically access them. This means you will need to have a system in place to avoid "stale inventory."

If you have your own products (not using a factory), you will need to make sure everything is packed and ready to go before you send it to Amazon. You need to pack your trinkets in whatever array you expect to sell them on the website. They will need to be inside boxes, ready to ship, too, before you send them off to Amazon. If you are going to be using a supplier factory, you should make sure to communicate to your supplier that your product will need to be ready-to-ship individually. That is unless you will be taking the shipments directly to your own facilities and packing them before sending them on to Amazon. That case, however, is probably going to cost you most unless you have some kind of highly streamlined, proprietary packing process. You can also pay Amazon for certain services, which will be covered below.

The next step is getting your products to Amazon. You can contract with one of their preferred carriers, which includes over 20 different companies. You can take your choice (just ask your current carrier if they are an Amazon partner). If you prefer to contract with a non-partner, you will not only miss out on the discounts: if you are shipping truckloads (literal truckloads, not figurative truckloads), you will need to make an appointment for the delivery to their warehouses. Amazon does not haphazardly receive product from anyone and store it in their facilities. They would not be so efficient if that is how they operated. The exact details you will need to read through yourself, as different types of shipments, different weights, products, and other considerations must be reviewed. Note Amazon will not fulfill orders on flammable liquids/solids and aerosols. That may seem irrelevant and commonsensical, but if you are selling certain cosmetic products, they will fall under this category. Just make sure the guidelines match up with your product. Furthermore, certain products can be listed and sold on Amazon, but Amazon will not store or ship them. You need to make sure your product does not fall into this latter category, too.

You may wonder how Amazon keeps track of all those packages it receives. Some of the more innovative ideas include using RFID chips and scanning incoming trucks – why take time and employees to confirm an incoming shipment when a truck rolling through the door can achieve the same thing and never require more than a few deciwatts of electricity? There is a whole area dedicated to finding efficiencies in such processes. However, for you, they will use barcodes. They use those barcodes to associate everything. This means you will need to have labels on each and every package you send to Amazon lest it gets lost in the synchronized chaos. These are the Amazon-specific labels you will find on any shipment you receive from them. You may do this yourself, or you may contract with Amazon to do it for you (for a fee, of course). On the other hand, if your products are generic and can be sold interchangeably with other sellers' merchandise, you can choose the "stickerless, commingled inventory" method. This can only occur if your product has a barcode already on it (such as a UPC or ISBN), which Amazon will scan. They will then place your product in among other sellers' inventory, and customers will get the same product. You will need to focus a lot on marketing and customer driving in order to get the sale under your name and not your competitor.

Currently, if you would like Amazon to "prep" your products for shipment (which means bagging or bubble wrapping them), you will pay $0.50 to $1 for standard sizes and up to $2 for oversized items. Labelling is generally $0.20, and the labeling is the Amazon label (not the UPC or other such scannable code!). Your products must have a scannable label on them in order to qualify for Amazon's labeling service. Note that this is a per-item cost and, if you are selling large quantities of small items, that cost will add up quickly. It might be worth your while to get your supplier to label them or at least another third-party. You can get the labels to add from Amazon for free. You just need to print and apply them.

One of the main advantages of having a company like Amazon to do your warehousing is that you can ship product around the country and have fast shipping times to your customers whether they live in New York City or Redwood City (that's in California). Amazon even notifies you that the difference for expedited shipping cut-offs between the East and West coasts can be as much as three hours. Well, if you use FBA, you can split up your inventory and send shipments all over the country. Furthermore, if you just want to drop your shipment to one location, Amazon will redistribute it for you (there is, of course, a fee).

Depending on your amounts, you can send them single pieces (small parcel delivery), or you can ship them by the literal truckload. Either way, you will need to have FBA labels on them as well to ensure Amazon knows the product is from you and that you want it warehoused. Pick up is available as well as the option to drop your product off at a designated shipping center.

They have the instructions on how to prep if you will be doing it yourself. If you are doing it yourself, make sure you have suffocation warning labels on your bags (for items that require bags). Remember, customers will not only be thinking of your product, but they will be associating it with Amazon. Neglecting to have a suffocation warning on the bag could cause issues for the company, and they have taken measures to prevent such problems (namely not accepting your packing standards if you don't have bags with the required label).

As for labeling, you can print your labels. They suggest a thermal or laser printer to avoid smearing. Smeared bars are not readable and hence cannot be processed. A company like Amazon will not have someone punching in the numbers on your label. All the sizes and placement locations are available on the website.

Once you have shipped your merchandise in, you can manage it from their online portal. Amazon provides an easy-to-use tool that will help you track your inventory. You can see how much is on its way to the fulfillment center, how much is available to customers, and how much is there but cannot currently be sent to customers (perhaps it must still be labeled, or a customer has purchased it, but payment has not yet cleared). You cannot directly manage the inventory (per package), so you will need to rely on good management to avoid paying storage fees while your product just sits in the warehouse taking up space.

Now that you know how to set everything up let's take a look at which products are best to sell (don't worry if yours isn't there, you can still sell) and how to get suppliers.

CHAPTER FOUR

SOME PRODUCTS ARE BETTER THAN OTHERS

As mentioned in a previous chapter, certain products are good for FBA and others not so much. Certain items are also restricted for FBA and cannot use this service. The majority of everyday products, however, can use the service and may be good candidates for the service. First and foremost, a manufactured product is simply a better plan than a unique product. If something is high-priced and high-quality, it may not benefit from the speed and logistical prowess of Amazon.

Josh Shogren, on his website, has a complete outline of his journey to build a business through Fulfillment by Amazon. His website, passionintopaycheck.com, is an archive and treasure trove for those looking to break into the industry. One of his posts talks about which products are best for this type of service. His tips include having a relatively inexpensive product, it being lightweight, no brand name competitors, hard-to-break items, a product that is easily related to other products, and repeat-sale items. He includes some others, but these are the ones I find to be most important. There are various reasons to focus on such products, with the main points from my own observations outlined below.

The inexpensive product is important because it allows people to not think much before buying, especially when it is lightweight too. That allows it to be tucked away in bigger orders for free, even to non-Prime users. If you have a product that people want, but is more likely they will purchase it if it is a low price. With the Small and Light program, you can be sure your product will be enticing to all Amazon customers, not just the Prime users.

Furthermore, if you have a repeat business item, you can expect your customers to return. That means you just need to get your customers to come once; then they will order again and again. Of course, you need to have a quality product (or sell it very, very cheaply) if you want such business. However, it helps build a business if you are confident you will have cash flow every period (whatever your period is) to rely upon.

Another important aspect of your product is for it to be easily related to other products. If you want to make a major business out of this, you will need to sell more than one thing. Once customers know your name, they will be more likely to buy from you again. If you start branding products that are related, it is easier for you to expand. If you want to have a very diverse set of products, that is possible, but people will not associate your name with your product category as often. If you sell similar products, or at least related products, your brand name will be associated more strongly with your category. If you just sell a couple, lesser-known items in several categories, the people shopping in Category A will not expect to look for your brand in Categories B and C. If your business is already built around highly diverse product sets, no worries. If you already have the customers, FBA can still help you immensely. On the other hand, if you are just getting into commerce and want to start out with FBA, it is advisable to stay within one product category.

Shogren also suggests products that are hard to break and having no brand name competitors. The latter is more important in my view because established brands already have serious marketing working on their side. If you happen to be one of those established brands, then you can disregard this tip. However, there will definitely be those among the readership who are starting out, and, if possible, enter product areas that have few brand name competitors. If you are trying to compete with L'Oréal, you will have a hard time convincing new customers yours is better, especially since the customer cannot see it first-hand at a store.

The suggestion to have hard-to-break items is not to be taken lightly. However, I find this to be much less of a consideration than the other points. All companies should strive to have high-quality items that do not break easily. However, as you will not be handling the returns and customer service yourself, it is not a huge burden to you if sometimes your product breaks. Of course, if your product breaks constantly, you won't be able to keep any customers, and bad publicity will spread much faster than good. So be aware that, as a general business rule, one should have a decent product; but that should not be a deal breaker for you.

You will also need to choose a product that has a reliable supplier base. Something too unique will be difficult to fulfill. If you happen to be manufacturing it yourself, make sure to have a scale-up plan in place in the event your business grows rapidly. There are few worse things in the retail world than customers going to competitors because you can't produce sufficient supply. If your handmade products are still high-volume enough to merit using FBA, you may want to consider raising your prices if your product is selling quickly. Avoiding out-of-stock messages on your product is essential to keeping customers, but especially so on a market like Amazon. If you are the only retailer of Product X in a small town with the next retailer a 75-mile drive away, you can afford to be out of stock sometimes. On Amazon, the next retailer is a few keystrokes and mouse clicks away, and having something out-of-stock even for a few hours can cause customer loss. Remember that many people shopping on Amazon are in it predominantly for convenience, and it certainly is not convenient to be required to return to the site later to order a product.

Finally, and most importantly, it is important to have something that can justify the use of FBA. Large, expensive, or unique items can still use FBA – Amazon isn't going to turn down your money because you make a loss – but they are not particularly suited to this business model. You will be paying large fees for the handling not only to your shipping company but also to Amazon to move your items around their warehouses. Another aspect to consider is the profit margin. If your product has razor-thin margins, there are two possibilities: Amazon will help you streamline your business and actually increase your profit, or it will eat into it. Only if Amazon is more efficient than your process will it increase your profits. Most likely Amazon will be more efficient, but if you only have a few sales a week, you probably won't see any appreciable savings. Hence this would not be an avenue for you (unless you have other reasons such as customer service to enroll).

In conclusion, the ideal product is one that is cheap and lightweight. After those two points are fulfilled, it is great to have something that is purchased regularly, easily scalable and/or relatable, and preferably having few competitors. Again, do not be discouraged if your product does not fit this category. Amazon's FBA can work just as well for your product if you are turning over enough merchandise to justify the use of FBA. If you only ship a few units a month, and they will incur high handling fees, though, perhaps you ought to look elsewhere. This is a model best suited to mass produced items that have a higher turnover.

CHAPTER FIVE

SOME SUPPLIERS ARE BETTER THAN OTHERS

Now that you have an idea of what kind of product to sell, you will need to find someone to make it for you. If you already make it yourself, then you can skip this chapter, as it mostly includes information on the search for suppliers and how to work with them. Of course, you might be able to get a few tips and pointers from it, and it won't take you too long.

If you are reading this, luckily for you, you speak the language of international commerce (English). Speaking the language of your supplier can go far, and it might be worthwhile to invest some time in at least learning some basic greetings. If you don't already speak the language, don't expect to be business fluent anytime soon, though. Using English only is perfectly acceptable, though, as most firms who work internationally will have some representatives that can speak English (otherwise they would have a hard time doing business with an array of countries).

If you already have a factory producing your wares, then you already know how to get your shipments to the United States (if they're produced elsewhere) and how much everything costs. You can use those figures to start selling on FBA. You should take a look at Amazon's fees for labeling and whether you meet the requirements (i.e., barcoded products). You should also ask your supplier if they offer any services for labeling (with the Amazon label). If they will label it, great. If not, then you could try finding a third-party labeler or just work with Amazon to label your products. You could do it yourself, too, if you don't have huge volumes or if you don't mind hiring a couple of employees you could still manage it yourself. It may be more cost-effective to get your factory to label it, though, as they can then ship it directly to Amazon. And remember, these factories are likely producing large quantities of product and shipping them on large cargo ships – they will have a better deal than you. Shipping it from your factory to your place of business to Amazon just adds one extra layer of shipping costs.

If you do not already have a factory, how can you find one? One great place to start is Alibaba.com. Ali Baba is the name of an Arabian folk character, but it is also the name of the world's largest site for commerce interaction. A few years ago, the company (out of China) made a big splash in the financial news as its IPO on the US markets was the largest ever tech IPO at the time. This company does a gargantuan volume of trade and is where you can find suppliers. They also run a banking arm, but you won't need to worry about that.

Alibaba is not one of the largest companies in the world for no reason. It is based in China, sells to the Chinese market, and allows Chinese firms to connect to the world. China itself is a huge and ever-growing (Often at dizzying levels) market. But you will not be selling to the Chinese (partially because Amazon FBA only allows listings on the US, Canadian, and Mexican marketplaces at the moment). How can you take advantage of the Chinese industrial juggernaut?

Using Alibaba, you can connect with suppliers inside and outside China. They have English listings, and you can usually contact them in English. It would be helpful if you or an employee can speak Chinese, as they will likely be more receptive to Chinese speakers than those who cannot. As China is not the only country with factories, you can filter the results based on the region. If you feel more comfortable with a North American supplier, you will find them. However, note that China or other countries known for lower-priced manufacturing will likely beat any North American or European supplier on price. Quality and reliability will need to be assessed on an individual basis. That can easily be achieved through an inspection of a sample. Keep in mind that the sticker that says "Made in ..." will carry weight with a lot of customers, too. However, often it is not possible to buy some of the cheaper products in countries that have a higher reputation in manufacturing.

On the site, there are several ways to avoid being scammed, but you still need to do your own, outside research once you find your supplier (or a pool thereof). This is where foreign languages may be more beneficial, as you might be able to find native-language reviews from other companies using them. Alibaba offers several filters you can use to avoid scams and find your product faster. Their Gold Supplier program will vet the supplier to a degree, and the supplier has to pay for the designation. Be aware this is a paid designation. Right on the search results page, you can see how long they have been a Gold Supplier. The search results page also generally includes Region, the total revenue, and the main markets in which the supplier is active. It also gives a response rate. It also gives you the terms of the Trade Assurance if there is any. This basically gives you an idea of the upper limit of the actual dollar amount the company will ensure will reach you. If you are buying a large quantity and the price is high, you will need to remember accidents do occur at sea, and if you lose your cargo but had no assurance or your own insurance, you will lose that money.

The Supplier's Page

Once you click on a supplier, you will be taken to a group of sites that help you better determine if this is the correct one for you. It will give you the year established and the number of employees, which can be helpful in determining whether a company is legitimate or not. Moreover, there may be a little "verified" phrase next to certain aspects, which means someone has been onsite and verified the claims – this just reassures you that you are not working with a paper company. There is usually a product categories tab and a contacts tab. That product categories tab will be helpful if you plan to scale out later. Once you establish a good business relationship with this supplier, you may want to use them again in the future to offer different products under your brand (remember relatable products are ideal). However, each supplier has their own group of sites, so certain aspects differ from supplier to supplier.

You should certainly contact the supplier to start a conversation. Not only can you get better terms by negotiating, but you can also perform your due diligence. You would not work with a company you didn't know and send thousands or hundreds of thousands of dollars to an unknown bank account, would you? You should not do that here just because you found a Gold Supplier with Trade Assurance that is verified by Alibaba. This is a business. If you feel uncomfortable working with a specific supplier for any reason, you are not obligated to do so. Take your money elsewhere.

Once you have established this is the supplier with whom you want to work, you can make a purchase. You will need to follow the instructions for each supplier; sometimes you must send money in a certain way (to a certain bank account) to qualify for the Trade Assurance if it is offered. You will need to know your shipping method (if more than one is offered) and the trade terms. These terms are known as Incoterms (INternational COmmercial Terms), and they govern the legal framework surrounding the shipping industry: who takes responsibility for what and where? A full explanation of the terms is outside the scope of this text, but you can find them (informally) on Wikipedia, where there is even a nice summary chart, and the enforceable, formal terms at the International Chamber of Commerce's website. It is important to understand the terms offered to you because it will dictate your responsibilities and where you assume the risk. You don't want your shipments tied up at a Chinese or American port because you didn't know you needed to get clearance. Or worse, you didn't purchase insurance because you thought the supplier was at-risk until unloading. However, the terms stated you took responsibility for loading of the cargo; now your products are at the bottom of the ocean and uninsured (this would be akin to you taking your cash, putting it in a box, and dropping it in the ocean).

The Product Page

The product page itself will give you information on that specific product and give you details for it. It can be daunting if you are starting out in a new product category and don't know all the aspects of a product. That would be your bonus to discover what information is important for your product. There are filters everywhere to help you get a better understand of that company's product. You should take some time to review the various filters from every supplier you find worth your time. Certainly, it is impossible to list all the filters and often they won't even apply to you, but transaction levels and markets are usually helpful to determine if this company is able to supply a large order and if your market takes a lot of orders. If your market does not, there are a few causes: there is no demand, there are better suppliers for your region, or, if you are lucky, there is demand, but no one is filling it yet. Of course, as this is only the market information for this particular product you will need to do more research to determine if there is demand. This is just one way the information presented to you can tip you off to a new product avenue that will make you a lot of money.

Here you can also see the amount the supplier can get to you, usually by month. That will determine whether they have enough capacity to cover your business. You can also see things like price per unit, shipping costs, and delivery times. The latter is important for your inventory management and avoiding that dreaded 'out-of-stock' banner on your product. If you are selling a technical product (say, photovoltaic panels), you can find the specifications here. Anything you think is missing should be a flag, but only a pink one, not a red one. You should ask the supplier about this aspect. That is why communication is important. Sometimes you may be looking for something that the industry does not generally find as important as you do.

Organizing your Suppliers and Contacting Them

It is a good idea to have a spreadsheet to organize your suppliers. It is likely that you will find more than one possible suppliers. Create columns corresponding to what you find important. I include name, country of origin, price per unit, whether they have various verifications and other verified identifiers, and their email address or contact method. Once you have a list, you should contact each one and ask for their terms. The most important terms are which payment methods they accept, if they can supply you (whether you are looking for large quantities or small), and what the shipping terms (Incoterms) are. You will also want to find out how much they are willing to negotiate on price. They may advertise one price and offer you another depending on your requirements. This is another area where you can leverage any foreign language skills – people will always prefer talking to business prospects in their native language. However, if you are not business fluent, it is advisable to stick to English. You won't be able to negotiate or make contracts if you are not business fluent, so it is not advisable to attempt.

Once you have it whittled down to a couple of suppliers, ask for samples. This will help you determine the quality of the product before you make a large purchase. If your supplier refuses, they are not your supplier. Especially if you are buying smaller, cheaper products, receiving a few samples should not be a problem. After you have found the best supplier, you can start getting shipments. Hopefully, at this point you already have your Amazon Seller's account set up, and FBA already arranged. That way you can have your supplier send the product directly to Amazon and start fulfilling your customers' orders as soon as possible.

By and large, these listings on Alibaba are companies that have invested time and resources into research and a manufacturing base. They simply want to make money just like you do. You need to be alert and conscious that scams do exist, but if you do your due diligence, communicate often and clearly, and Alibaba has vetted them, you will likely have a good experience with your supplier. Also, Alibaba is a great way to connect with suppliers, especially in the Asian manufacturing region. This is not the only site, though. You only need to do a simple Google search to find them. Aside from Alibaba, there are Global Sources, Made in China, and the China Sourcing Blog can all be leads. Global Sources offers reports you can read to get a better understand of the market. Trade shows are also a good place to go if you have the time and money. You can meet suppliers in person, which will help build the relationship. Similar aspects that apply on Alibaba will apply on these sites and events: communication, minimum order quantity, unit prices, verifications and trust, shipping and payment methods, and legal responsibilities. You don't have to stick to Alibaba if you find another, better B2B platform or even if you stumble upon a social media post to a great supplier. As mentioned in the introduction: the internet and globalization are bringing people together all the time. While commerce may seem highly automated and human-free, you will notice as you work with these suppliers and your customers that they are, indeed, humans too, and you will be communicating with them and following human-generated leads more and more.

CHAPTER SIX

TO CONTINUE OR TO EXIT

This chapter will help you determine your future on FBA. You may read this chapter when you are first starting to help you think about your exit strategy. You should also return here after you have built your business and have a decent cash flow from it. The decision to stay in business yourself or sell is a personal one, but I will try to help you along in the decision. It is highly dependent on your own circumstances and whether you still have the time and passion. In the future, once you have built a solid brand on FBA, you may want to sell your position for a tidy, known sum and move on to something else. It seems that as more and more businesses move online, and many smaller ones use major resources like Amazon, it will become more common to buy and sell such businesses.

Anyone who has built a business from the ground up will tell you that it takes hard work, and you will often have a connection to your company. It is, at least partially, your own creation. Three major considerations for you to decide whether to stay on or exit are your passion for the business, how much money it makes you, whether you want to pursue something else.

PASSION

If you still enjoy working with your business, you may not want to part with it. If, on the other hand, you have found a new interest, it may be time to let go. You can continue to build out your business into other areas if they attract your attention. However, you should note that it may be difficult to break into another category, even if you have an established brand. The same ideas from previous chapters apply, even if you have a loyal customer base and a solid brand.

It is sometimes hard to see exactly where a business stands and exactly where it might lead. The first thing to know is how you created the business yourself, and it is most important to continue it because you want to see the business succeed. It is not about moving forward through the force and stress of the world, but it is about waking up each day knowing that you accomplished something that you wanted to do.

Before you make any decision to change the path or move into a different place in life, look at the reasons for why you got to this place. How you were originally motivated and why you decided to take that first step to creating the business. Not everyone decides to just start a project like you have in the business. Because of this, it is all about your passion towards accomplishing the next great part of the project.

Passion drove the business and helped you build your business from the start. If you lose your passion, there is little reason to continue to the pursuit. You can also sell parts of the business but retain a stake so you can keep an eye on it while retaining some of the profits. Just like everything else discussed here, it is business, and it is negotiable.

MONEY

If you have a solid brand, you may be generating decent, steady profits from it and don't want to give it up. That is perfectly fine. Note that others will also see those steady profits and offer you years-worth of (discounted) cash flow in a single payment. If you happen to be interested in another venture and need money for it, this is a great way to free up some of your cash (especially in inventory without liquidation and in future profits that simply cannot be taken any other way). Many firms that make such acquisitions will want to absorb your brand, so you should be aware that, if you do sell, you may be losing control of your creation. That is a personal decision.

Furthermore, it is important to know what kind of future you want. If your business brings you good income every month with minimal work, it may be worthwhile to keep it. Even if it only generates a little income but is easy to manage, you may like that known (though surely not guaranteed!) cash flow provided by the business. On the other hand, if it generates a lot but requires significant time investments, you may find it better to sell and let someone else do the work while still reaping a percentage of those future profits.

The role of money in the sale or continuation of business is, therefore, dependent on two factors: your personality and the demands of the business. If your personality still meshes well with the demands, then by all means continue. You will still love the business and want to grow it. Or even if you don't love it, it might bring you money for something you don't mind doing. However, if your business and your personality have diverged, it is likely best to take your profits and start something new.

OTHER PURSUITS

While these considerations are all tightly intertwined, you will need to look at each one closely and do some soul searching. Do you have other projects you want to work on? Do you want to start a different business? What about moving into a new area under a new name? If you have grand ambitions but lack the cash, selling the business is definitely the way to go. If you just need a little financing, keeping the business and employing a few people to run it may be a better plan. You will free yourself from the daily tasks but still get a cash flow, which you can use to finance your other projects.

Of course with the amount of passion and time you have put into the business, the thought of letting it go can be hard. Not only can that happen, but the idea of letting go of a single part of a business can become overwhelming. Since any single business, whether large or small, has to build itself from the start, it is hard to think about letting it go. It is easy to build it up until it has multiple parts and it is easy to continue going once it has been made. Before making any rushed decisions on what to do, think about how important it is to you. Is this business, your dream at one point, something you want to walk away from for good? It is also important to think about how it all came to be. Think about all the different parts that have come to be over the years. Think about what you've learned about business and how even on the worst days, you still kept going. Doing all of this seems like more difficult work than it truly is, but just follow the steps below to figure out how to negotiate different parts of the business.

First, take a look at the components of the business. Make a list of all the things that are continually built or run through on a daily or weekly basis. This can be updates on a website, advertising to find more customers or funding for more resources.

Sometimes it can become a hassle to run all these areas at the same time, so people will negotiate removing one part of their business for another person to handle. It is nothing bad to do; it simply forms a partnership with another area in order to bring a higher profit margin and more focus on your own areas of the business.

Second, take a look at the profit margins for the business. This is to see if the business is making enough money to satisfy yourself in living. The best way to find out is by making a chart of what money is being gained and what money is being lost. To figure out the money that is being gained, make a list of all the areas that are gaining profit. For example, selling products to consumers, getting money from advertising, or negotiating deals of stocks or investments. Write down all of these numbers in an excel sheet and label them all to be a positive value. Next, make a list of all the areas that you are losing profit from. These are the places where you are spending money to gain resources for the business. For example, shipping costs, employee costs, material costs, website costs, or fuel in traveling cost. Write down all the values in an excel sheet and label them as a negative value. Add the positive numbers and the negative numbers together to see the final number overall for how well everything has done up to this present moment. If it is well in the positive, then you are good. If it is deep in the negative, then you may want to consider making some major changes or possibly selling the business. If it's not too bad of a value, but a little low, then it might best to think about allowing someone else to control another part of the business. For example, allowing Amazon to work with the shipping and storage of the products means that they could focus on the product itself as you focused on gaining more revenue from the website through advertisements. Being able to see the overall specs of how well or how bad the business is doing can help you to see which side you stand on. Any part of a business can be negotiated, so there is no concern to getting rid of parts of it. Sometimes, you may have to find another source of help in order to gain more profit and more connections with other people. But, if you feel that you have put too much energy and too much stress into the business, and you have only gained a small amount of income, it might be best to consider a different option for your business.

Third, take a look at the growth of the business through the buyers. See how many people are looking at the product, buying the product, or having the potential to buy the product. Doing this will help you to find out how much your business is increasing in order to show the potential it has to grow towards higher levels of success. To chart this all out, first take a look at the number of people you have encountered in your business each day, week, month, or year. The amount of time you wish to chart is your choice. If you are selling a product for a kitchen or office, it might be best to chart it out to be either a week or a month. If you are selling furniture, it might be best to chart it out to be either a month or a year. The next step is to find all the people that have encountered your business from day one. Split them into three categories: people who bought, people who viewed the product, and people who showed interested in the product (those who liked the product, left a review, or saved the product for later). When looked at the people who bought the product, list how many people bought the product each week. Set up a graph with a horizontal line (X-direction) for the time in weeks and then a vertical line (Y-direction) with the bottom of the line connecting to the very left of the horizontal line. The vertical line will be the number of people who are accounting for. To find out how high you need the numbers in the graph to go, look at how many weeks your company has existed and then look at the highest number of customers that you received, these should both be the highest points of the graph. For example, if you have had twenty customers one week over a fifteen-week period, you may want to make the graph go to thirty people on the vertical line and then twenty on the horizontal line. It is best to leave that extra space if you wish to continue going on in the business. Once you have plotted the points matching each week to the number of customers, draw a line to connect the points. Continue going until you are done with the three different categories of people. You can either have three different graphs or three different lines on one graph.

With these different points to compare, it is easier to see how much your business has increased and how much profit has been made from the start. Since things can get overwhelming with what to negotiate in the business, these graphs can help you to see the popularity or the increasing income to make a decision. More money is spent at the beginning to cover the expense of growing the business, and there would be fewer people at the start with a smaller amount of advertising and less time for the product to be seen. For example, during the first week of the business, the product has had no chance for advertising, no chance on the website since it is new, and lots of money has been spent on the resources to get the product completed for the business. Once the third week has come, more people might have seen the product and decided to buy it. While more resources would have to be bought to create more products, it is not as many products. Beginning with one hundred products, you would have to spend the money on the resources to create all of those products. If only three were sold at the beginning, then you would only need to spend the money to create three products instead of another one hundred products.

Overall, it is important to keep track of the amount of income that has developed through the business, and it is important to keep track of an increase of customers. With more positive values and more of an increase, it becomes easier to see how much of the business should be kept and how much should be in the control of another partner. It is important to know the passion you have for the accomplishments in the business, but it is also important to know about the amount of energy you put into the project. The more you put into the project and the less you get out of the project, the more stressed overall you will become.

This consideration obviously is dependent on whether you have further pursuits in mind. These do not have to be career or business pursuits, either. If you want to spend more time with your family or take a couple of years to sail around the world, you probably won't be able to tend to your business. In this care, you need to plan your exit strategy. You don't want to kill off your creation. Let it live in the hands of others.

EXIT TYPE

As you may have noticed, there is more than one exit method. You can outright sell the company and let someone else take over all the operations and profits. This is best if you need a large sum of cash or if you just want to get out of the sector altogether. Usually, an acquiring company will perform several calculations, but one includes a Discounted Cash Flow analysis. This looks at the expected profits from future sales and calculates their current value based on interest rates and other metrics. If your company expects to do well in the future, this could mean you will receive a lot more than just a year or two worth of income from the sale. That money can immediately be plowed into another project or used for that two-year sailing vacation.

You don't have to leave the business entirely, though. If you still want some control, you can work out deal terms that let you continue to make decisions, but most of the daily operations are taken care of by another company. This will often include having diminished profits, as the other company will want some of the profits to take over. You can even set up a system that gradually transfers control to another entity with a stop clause. If your company starts to do better, you may want to stop the sale of your company and buy back the portion you already sold. Contracts can be creative.

Another option, if you don't want to let much at all, is to hire employees to take care of the business. The difference here is that the employees are not investing in the company to make money. They expect a steady paycheck and some benefits. This will allow you to keep a lot more of the profits and simply pay someone to take over operations of the business. Of course, you could profit share with your employees, which will attract different types of applicants than if you just pay a steady salary.

As you can see, you have several options and considerations for your exit. Only you can decide which is the best method to exit if that is indeed your decision. There is no right answer, but some strategies will work better with your current and future goals and desires than others. Even if you are not planning on selling now, you may want to field some offers to see how much you can sell for. You may be surprised at the result and decide selling is better than staying in now. Do not rush, though. Any sale or transfer of control you plan will need to be thoroughly reviewed. Just like there are scammers instead of suppliers, you will find people who are not genuine when you want to sell. It is harder to be scammed when you are selling than when you are buying because you already have control over your own assets; however, you can still lose your assets legally if you are not careful. Just as you may have used Amazon because you didn't know how to program, if you are not a lawyer, you would benefit from hiring one. Especially for something as complicated as a business sale, it is a good idea to have at least one set of legally-knowledgeable eyes looking through the content.

CHAPTER SEVEN

MARKETING AND PROMOTING THE PRODUCT

As you can see, there is a lot of work that goes into running and even beginning a business standpoint. Not only is it about finding the right product, but it is also about finding the balance between passion, income, and success. Once you are able to find that balance, it becomes easier to follow through with the business and obtain more levels of achievements. One of these achievements is managing the seller competition and being able to get more sales against the competition.

When trying to see how you have worked through the ranges of the competition, try to look at how much of your own sales for the product have dropped, look at how much the consumers have gone through and turned towards the competition, and then look at the pressure for maintaining the price. This means keeping the price steady for people to continue buying the product and having them feel as if purchasing the product was worth it. No one wants to buy a fifty-dollar product that is actually only worth five dollars. Yes, there are many prices involved in the overall price of the product, but people look around for the best deal. They will buy any off brand and any other product besides yours if the competitor's product has a better and lower price.

While you have been reading through these chapters to see how you can improve your own business strategies through Amazon FBA, it is important to continually research the different levels of competition. See how you can find the other buyer's cost and benefit. There are many other places that involves other levels of sellers and retailers that are all experiencing the same thing. Whether they have been working for years or days, they all have to go through the research of competitors and follow through the seasons of the year. It is through all four seasons that the competition for products and the level of consumers change, so the work always continues throughout the place.

With the connection to the Amazon FBA sellers, they work differently since they know the amount of experience and knowledge it takes for them to get through the product ranges of competitors. Being able to sell a product on Amazon is sort of like selling a product in the wild jungle. It is more about how your product stands out in the strength of advertising and how consumers see your product first will give you the advantage of selling the most. A basic survival of the fittest mentality since it is more about getting people to see the product rather than making the perfect product. The question is, how does Amazon do this differently to the point where they stand out from everyone?

The truth is that Amazon sellers are nothing like the others that run around only going door to door. They are the most successful sellers that have been able to go themselves into people of online retail that treat selling products on Amazon like they are trading at the stock market. Because of this, Amazon has had an increase in the amount of focus on their prices and convenience from the consumer rather than focusing on the value and selection of the product. They have been able to become traders that take their own strategic and analytical approach to their own stock portfolios. These same sellers have also been able to apply this technique towards their own inventories to keep track of all the products in their own company.

In Amazon's old retail model, they were loyal to retailers, they were relatively stable throughout the seasons, they had an SKU selection from the manufacturers, and their inventory investments would take only a few annual turns. This was how they first operated and how they were first able to go through the system of retail. It is true that they were able to take these first strategies and used them in the new model, but they learned through the system and how to get through it all differently. In their second system in the improved retail model, they were able to focus on having the lowest prices and fastest delivery times, they would constantly change the prices of all their items based on the amount of supply and demand, the commodities would be valued based upon the market value, and they would be constantly changing their own diversified portfolio.

Part of these strategies of changing into the different models of the business is that they would be successful sellers that work for Amazon FBA to help them scale their own business. The more experienced sellers in this strategy know that the merchant fulfillment programs are able to take away from the margins, the ability to pack efficiently, the ability to ship efficiently, and the cost of millions of dollars in investments. Merchant fulfillment takes these parts away as they require many different variables in the business, and they require more effort than other places. These sellers for Amazon FBA are able to save time in the company by not worrying completely about the logistics of the situation as they choose to be more focused on gaining a competitive advantage. Through this advantage, they work to gain access to the millions of other Prime customers that signed up to Amazon for the convenience factor of the products. They continually are valued customers that work to hold more and expect the same satisfaction each time they purchase an item online.

To gain more of the competitive advantage with other companies, it is important to create your own winning portfolio and create your own bets or risks in the business. The third party sellers in the Amazon unit sales make up about forty percent of the entire system. These sales are not evenly distributed among the different sellers. A few of them are used for making up a majority of the volume, and they are able to work with a stock trading model. They use their investments in more of a short-term focused theme, and they are more focused on getting the most profit from their own created portfolio. They are also less focused on what the manufacturers are presenting to them, and they are more focused on seeing the products driven inside the dynamics of the market.

These successful Amazon FBA sellers work to maintain the diverse portfolio of products and inventory levels that all depend on multiple different variables. This is done in order to reduce risk. Being able to make bets is the best way to make a sufficient sale. It can either be for all inventory or for a strategy decision that is designed for the stock of the competitors. In order to utilize the stock trading model, a seller needs to make the decisions by using a fact based data analytics program to create less of a risk and more profitable opportunities for the business. This can be done in excel spreadsheets or software. Either can be used, and it depends on the size of the business you are working towards. The most successful Amazon sellers share the same kind of unique traits that are required of the successful stock traders. There are five key steps that are involved in making a successful stock trader.

The first step is to have flexibility and focus in the business. Being able to focus on the investments that are in a high margin as the high volume is crucial to growing the business. The sellers with a poor performance will choose to focus on the lower volume inventory, and they will find themselves backup beyond a point of moving forward. They will be stuck. Even if a business has higher margins, they cannot successfully scale a business with a lower volume of products. Stock traders do not make a major profit from lower risk investments. They aim for high margin and high volume. One of the easiest ways to maintain and have a growing high volume and high margin is to sell the products with Amazon FBA. Trying to reach those levels by yourself and attempting to reach all the areas of fulfillment logic on your own will eventually create a higher ceiling that no individuals by themselves can reach. Reaching this stop in the business cause less profit to move through and more opportunities to leave your business. As for the flexibility in the focus, it is a very important factor in the business. Amazon sellers must be able to prepare for bad bets. They have to have a game plan in order to manage the bets with a certain amount of flexibility to provide a safety if things go wrong. Of course, mistakes happen all the time and people in business' will sometimes buy the poor product without thinking about it. Even some of the most seasoned stock workers of the FBA workers at Amazon sometimes make bad investments. While this happens, they are smart sellers that are able to see when a good or bad decision in an investment has been made. The most important part of this is that they will admit to making a poor decision. They will see that they made a wrong move, and they will move forward towards other more profitable ventures in other business projects. Poor investments made by people continually tie into the capital and have the potential of crippling the business. The smart and successful sellers or traders have to make adjustments in order to correct the bad decisions and learn from their own mistakes. Once this has happened, they are able to improve upon their future buying decisions for the business itself.

The second step is to have a balanced amount of discipline in the business. The successful sellers and traders in the Amazon FBA combine performance metrics with other forms of data analysis in order to build a large amount of long-term success in the business. These levels of discipline are the gross margin hurdles, the total inventory values, the stale inventory, the overall ratio of cash flow, the profitability analysis, delegation, risk management, cash flow management, and obtaining the road to long-term success. In the routine performance metrics, the gross margin hurdles area is all about maintaining a minimum gross margin benchmark. This comes after all of the Amazon FBA fees, and it is where you would begin to be interested in selling the product. The total inventory value is about how much you have been able to invest in the product in order to efficiently manage your business. It is about being able to know where the capital funding is allocated and being able to see where the budget profits stay. The stale inventory is the inventory that exists, have ninety days of the product existing, and it is what would be weighing the worth of the product overall. The inventory in the sales cash flow ratio will show how much cash flow needs to be generated in order to have a certain amount of sales. The profitability analysis is about the net impact of returns of a particular product. Without taking this into account, you might be blindly thinking that your product is doing well when it is actually failing.

The five areas of the routine performance metrics (gross margin hurdles, total inventory value, stale inventory, inventory for sales cash flow ratio, and profitability analysis) all add up together to move forward into the data-driven management with the delegation, risk management, and cash flow management. With these two paths together, a person is able to find themselves at long term success faster with more efficient profit value margins. Simply by following the definitions in the above routine performance metrics to see what stage your own business is at and where you would be able to carry forward in a profit margin, success will be able to come. While it does take time to find a certain amount of success, this way of success will work for the owner of the business through Amazon FBA.

The third step is excellent money management. Without the skill or action of money management or access to the profit capital, it is impossible to earn money for the business through trading stocks or running a successful Amazon business. It is important to focus on the cash flow and provide yourself with access to the working capital in order to have the ability to place orders and purchase the needed inventory to grow the business. Knowing the inventory to sales ratio for these product resources is crucial when looking for success in the business. This ratio directly relates to money management since you cannot efficiently manage a business without knowing the direction of your own profit capital. If all of your money is tied into bad investments, then you will begin to see a trend where you lose out on potential profits and will begin to potentially sink your own business in the process.

The phase of money management begins with the credit facilities and the working capital for the business. Here there are the vendor credit terms worth a net value of thirty, sixty, and ninety. There is allow the use and need of credit cards, term loans, and revolving credit statements. The credit in this business model of money management is one of the most important areas to remember. The most successful sellers in a business environment work to constantly develop access to the working capital, and they are also continually working to find places of credit for new investments through these few options. The first option is about the vendor credit terms where people look towards the manufacturers and ask for a net time of either thirty, sixty, or ninety days. These terms depend on what you have already built for yourself in the business and what you have built yourself in terms of a solid credit history with the retail business. The second option is through the work of credit cards. The credit cards like American Express Plum Card or Chase Ink are the cards that consumers look for since they have cash back rewards for small businesses. The third option is for the term loan and revolving credit statements. These include the Amazon lending program where Amazon is able to provide three to six months to repay the loan with interest. It also includes Kabbage for loans or getting the loans directly through your bank.

Using all of these options will allow the seller to plan ahead for the areas of high-velocity periods (such as Q4), and they will all help in managing a balance for yourself in a steady business platform. Most of the time, businesses are targeted towards the holiday seasons in order to see where many of the sellers are able to make their own profits throughout the year. As a general rule, the more upfront capital you have, the better your own ability to see a substantial profit becomes. More capital means more profit in the business. Any time a person chooses to borrow money from a corporation, it is important for them to look at future profits and wages to be sure that they are able to pay off the loan. Normally, sellers also choose to focus on profit through loans since they know how easy it is to fall into areas of debt with loans. They borrow money to be able to make more money in the future, but at the same time, they know that they are able to fall back into debt whenever they are trying to pay back the capital they borrowed.

The fourth step is the ability to be emotionally controlled. Some people is business say that it is all about making money instead of being right about everything. While this seems like a wrong statement to some people, it is important to not focus too much on the good buying decisions for the business. Sometimes, a good idea one moment may turn into a bad idea later on. If a seller is only looking at the good ideas each time without thinking about the influence of money, then they can actually turn out to make less of a profit. The most successful sellers are able to react to the bad investments in the same way that a stock trader would. They decide to use a rational response rather than stopping to get stuck on proving to everyone that they were right about the investments. Any buyers on the team as well must be able to be held accountable by using a set of transparent metrics. Doing this will allow them to manage the buyers objectively, and it will be able to place the whole team on the same line of expectations for the business.

The fifth step is simply the idea of patience. The consistent and sustainable growth in the business depends on time. The performance and the scale through iteration also depend on time. The gradual increasing exposure to risk happens over time as well. The most successful retailers use these ideas as they measure their growth by quarters or years sometimes. They rarely measure out the business on a week to week basis. The consistent and sustainable growth is one of the main keys to the long-term success. Being able to look at how the overall business is doing in the long term is an important term for growth. It allows for efficient growth rather than quick spikes through a specific product or a particular brand.

Similar to the conditions in the stock market, there are certain products and stocks that will continuously go up and down. The stocks might go down one day and then be up at higher levels than before for the next week. A person will not be able to assess the success of the project through a short time period in the business. Otherwise, they will be distracted by statistical noise. Another important point to realize is that it is important to have lots of patience when looking at the investments. Even if a person has multiple places of upfront capital, they still have to remain patient when looking to invest. The most successful sellers want to be sure that their strategies are working and being proven before placing their own bets on a project area. If you are able to start on more of a small scale and then prove that the product will have a high selling rate, then you will see that it is safe to continue reordering the resources for the products and sell at a higher volume. Either way, lots of patience in involving in the process of selling the product. One way to have more control of the situation is through marketing the product in different areas online. It is important to be widespread in order to reach the most number of people, and therefore, it is important to read through and research more strategies for marketing the product.

Strategies to Marketing the Product

Once you have gone through to successfully launch the product on Amazon, the next step is figuring out how to sell it and make a profit from it. While it takes work to get a product on Amazon, the same work continues in order to ensure that you will have the most amount of profit running through the business. You will first need to think about what kind of effective launching strategy you want for the product in order to rank your product as high as possible in the Amazon search engine.

The way that Amazon's product and sales algorithm works is through ranks. The more sales and reviews a product receives, the higher it will rank on Amazon. Once the product is ranked, then the product will gain more organic sales from many other kinds of Amazon products every day without you needing to do work each and every day. There are five main strategies to follow that people normally use to have their product stand out through Amazon. There are many products out there that people are trying to sell, and at the same time there are many people looking each and every day at Amazon for more products to buy.

The first strategy to use is giving away the products. This does not mean allowing the product to be free; it simply means that the product should be as low as one or two dollars. Early on when selling a product, it is more about the rank on Amazon rather than the profit gained. The more people that view and buy your product at that low price, the higher your rank will become on Amazon. This is a very simple and fast way to get a lot of sales and reviews in the company. In the Amazon Seller Central, people will have the option to set up the promotions, and they will be able to use coupon codes to use on the products. You can use this same feature to convince people that they are getting a great deal so that they can buy the product for only a couple dollars. Giving these coupons away to family, friends, and random strangers throughout the day will help to increase your rank in Amazon. Once they receive the product, ask them to leave a steady review as well. An honest review will help people to buy the product. When a person is looking to buy a product, they will prefer to know that the product was used by other people. Customers prefer to read product reviews from other customers. Of course, a company selling a product will always point out the positives and paint the picture that they have the best product on the market. Buyers want to know the practical reviews from other people just like them.

When you sell the product for a lower price, or you use these coupons to sell the product at a lower price, you may continue to break even or even begin to lose money. It all depends on the cost of the manufacturing of the product. If this is your first time selling a product on Amazon, it is recommended to sell a product that is inexpensive to make. Around five dollars or less in resources for each product is a good target to find yourself in. If your own product costs fifty cents to make from China, then selling the product for only one or two dollars will not cost you much. In which your product will begin to break even. But, if your own product costs ten dollars to make, every time you sell it at these low prices, you will lose around ten dollars each time. This is why choosing the right item to selling on Amazon is very important. You want to gain a rank in your product while not breaking the bank.

The second strategy to use is Amazon Ads. Anyone selling a product on Amazon should use Amazon Ads. By using these, the product will be seen by more people and in return, it will get more sales. This will give you more profits and a higher rating on your product. These ads can be found in the 'Campaign Manager' section in the Amazon Seller Central. At the beginning of this marketing strategy, people should choose to start off with 'Automatic' targeting in order to reach as many people as possible. The software will ask for you to set a daily budget as a payment for the advertising. The more you have in the daily budget, the more overall exposure the ads will get for your product. Once you get a couple hundred dollars from the Automatic targeting system, then move over to a 'Manual' targeting system for people to follow. This will give you the control for targeting keywords that relate to your product. If people begin to search desk chair, and you are selling those, then you can choose to advertise your product to those people who used those specific words in the search bar.

The third strategy to use is through Buview and Zonblast. These are two of the main resources that sellers on Amazon can use to help sell their product. The seller will be able to promote their product and sell their product through the help of these programs. Often times, people will be required to use a coupon code for the product as they search through and see a better deal. With these programs, the product is promoted on other people's lists as they are important for maintaining the success in business. They are not completely necessary, but they are helpful to spread the name of the product. A word of warning, though, when using either of these programs, be sure to reserve most of your inventory before using the service. If not, you put yourself at risk of losing all of your units rather quickly. In these programs, you will have to monitor your own inventory and keep track of how many products are being sold through the service. This is only as a safety to be sure that you are getting the most amount of money that you can through the service.

The fourth strategy to use is called Tomoson. This is a website that gives you access to many other bloggers from around the world. They would be able to see your product and buy it for themselves or promote the product to other followers and subscribers. One of the best parts about this website is that you are able to set it up for free and try it out. After doing that, you are able to list the product on the website and then watch as many dozens of bloggers receive the product and promote it through the site naturally. After this has been done, you will be required to give the product away at first in order to see the popularity of the item. Once the customers receive the product, they will be able to post a review of the product on their own blog and link the review over to Amazon. They can also create a YouTube video review on the product and link the video to Amazon. Otherwise, they would be able to post it on social media sites such as Facebook, Twitter, Pinterest, and Instagram. All of these strategies will allow the customer to leave an honest review for you on Amazon, and they will be able to talk about the product among their own followers.

Since the site Tomoson is free, it is about how much money you put into the site and how much you want to contribute to the bloggers. While you are giving away the product for free, it is important to realize how many people a blogger would be able to contact. The largest bloggers on the site will look at the product, but they will be more focused on the highest bidder. The more money you give to the bloggers, the more likely it is that they would be willing to spread your product to other people around the world. They might ask for only ten dollars, twenty dollars, and fifty dollars, but it is enough money to convince them for the favor of reviewing your product.

If their blog is large enough, they would be able to provide more advertising and more sales towards your product.

The fifth strategy is through Facebook. It might sound strange to turn to social media for selling the product, but the appearance of social media has grown over the years. Facebook is one of the main ways to sell your own Amazon products. There are many ways a person can use Facebook, and in this sense, they can set up Facebook ads in order to target a certain group of buyers. One way to build the Facebook fan page is by building a page for people that are interested in the niche. Then you would be able to launch the product on the fan page. Many people have had success through these pages. For example, someone selling fitness bands for workouts will want to reach out to people into fitness. By building up a fan page to almost four thousand likes from fitness enthusiasts in a few weeks, the advertisements for the product is able to begin. In order to build up this kind of page, it is best to target the people that enjoy fitness. Then it is important to provide a value to the product. Give a reason for why this product would be important for them to have. Since Facebook is a very powerful social media page, the same can be said for the other social media sites such as Pinterest, Twitter, and Instagram.

One of the ways that technology has changed today is through the presentation of the device. When someone receives a new phone, one of the first things they see when they turn it on is smartphone applications for social media. This is done for two main reasons. First, it is a kind of effort to help people quickly connect themselves to the world instead of waiting or forgetting to do so. Second, it is a promotion of the social media app itself in order to bring more popularity to the app and more business to the products on the apps. More and more people are moving through the web to connect to others. Businesses are able to see this trend and take advantage of the potential customer values. Some research has proven that seventy-two percent of people on the internet are also a part of social media. In addition to this number, about ninety-three percent of marketers are using social media for their own business.

In Amazon FBA, they have come up with more ways to direct the website traffic throughout the products in the Amazon stores. There are many groups of people that gather online that search the internet for bloggers and go through the daily task of seeing what their friends and family are doing with their lives. At the same time, these people are able to see advertising on the side, and they are able to potentially view your own product.

Mainly Pinterest and Facebook are good social media places to start out with in terms of advertising the product. They are a good platform for businesses to build a foundation upon and show their product to an intended targeted audience. These business people and marketers are using these platforms to direct the traffic flow of people to their product listing, and they are using the platforms to build a customer list for later on in the future. This form of listing is done using a site called 'leadpages.net' as it leads to directly potential buyers of sales and other coupon pages in exchange for their email address. This automated list can provide you with a continuous stream of income as they continue to roll out more products and offer more to the customers.

Selling a product on Amazon's platform means that the business is being built on someone else's land base. Since Amazon is overall in charge, we are the people that have to play by their rules. One of the main rules to follow is that the people who decide the product must be qualified Amazon customers. It is not a bad idea to sell on their platform; this is only a quick word of caution to be aware of. Knowing that a person is part of Amazon, they will most likely choice to return there for their products, and they will then be able to see your product. Because of this, Amazon is still a great place to connect with and be a part of. The number of views and online traffic they are able to bring to each single product is amazing. They are also very efficient with handling the products they have in their warehouses. What would normally take five years to build, they would be able to ramp and sell in about six months to a year.

Being able to use social media in the field of marketing will be able to allow this same traffic in Amazon to your own product. At the same time, you would be able to build a customer list in order to build a long lasting business foundation. On sites such as Pinterest, they have the 'Buy Button' in order to compete with Amazon. Facebook had the same innovation as they were nothing compared to the sellers through Amazon. When it comes to these different values of social media, it is best to consider building a personal page for the product so that people can search and share it for themselves. It would quickly be passed through the social media apps, and it would allow for a larger business advertising to be made.

Promoting Your Product

As one of the most popular websites in the world, Amazon continues to be seen as a great place to sell products. But, marketing, on the other hand, can become quite a challenge for people to solve. Seeing millions upon millions of products can be quite overwhelming to view or even think about. In order to turn one of the many fifty million visitors on Amazon to your own product, you have to understand how this worldwide business platform works worldwide with many different small business owners. Here are a few things to think about when getting starting in marketing.

First, think about Amazon as an ecommerce Website. Being able to build your own ecommerce website can become costly, and it can take up a lot of time. It is important to have a website like this, but it is a hard challenge to begin with when you are a small business owner. When working with Amazon, you will be able to use them like this website. You will have the benefits of selling on one of the most popular store sites online, even if you only have a small product or a small quantity of products to sell. As you continue to grow your business, you have the option to continue adding products to Amazon while expanding yourself to other sites as well.

Second, think about the kind of products that sell the most on Amazon. Since Amazon is a rather large site, many sellers will find themselves selling a product that many other people are trying to sell as well. It is important to notice that Amazon creates a single page for each product on the site. When all of the individual sellers on Amazon are marketing themselves on the same page, then they all get mixed together. If you are selling a product that twenty other people are also selling, the idea of making any kind of sale is low, especially if your product is not the cheapest option. The sellers with the best price for the buyers and selling history will have more control over what is called the 'buy box.' This means that the seller will be able to receive the sale more likely since they are listed under the 'add to cart' button. The other sellers of the same product are simply listed as 'other' and shown on a secondary page. If your name is on the secondary page, then it is most likely that you will not be able to make a quick sale. If your name is not on the front and center of the page, buyers may not see your product. Because of this, it makes sense to marginalize the competition through marketing your own kind of unique product or simply reselling something unique made by another person. You have to remember that there are many experts in the market on Amazon that tell people it is not a good idea to sell media related products such as videos, books, or music on the site. They are only trying to help you make money and bring the most customers to your product.

Third, remember to price the product very carefully. There are many cases where businesses will slow down their own profit margins when selling an item on Amazon in the hopes of jumpstarting a sale. Some people have products that should be sold at a lower price to gain more popularity than cash, but if you are looking to make a decent profit quickly, it is best to price your product fairly. If you are in the middle of which side to choose, selling at a low price or selling at a fair price, it is best to then sell the product at a fair price. If it does not work out at the beginning, then put the product on a lower price margin to gain more popularity with the product to increase future sales. Also remember to factor in the monthly fee for selling the product on Amazon. The shipping costs themselves will help to provide a basic price for the product itself.

Fourth, think about how to sell more products through the product ads on Amazon. Since Amazon offers their own advertising system and program, they are able to stand out farther than Google AdWords. Using this kind of program on Amazon is a smart idea if you do not want to the product you are selling to end up on a competitor's site. This program in advertising will help you to take advantage of Amazon's traffic system. Every time an advertisement is clicked on, you will be charged per click. The prices for each ad will vary depending on the category that you choose. The more popular categories can cost more than one dollar per click while some others are only pennies for each click. Being able to set up these ads is a rather quick process on Amazon, but some of the categories do require a section of pre-approval before the actual ads are posted.

Fifth, take advantage of marketing the product on other sites as well. To increase your own level of success in selling on Amazon, it is best to produce your own product content on other social media channels and blog sites. Post on Facebook about your product, post the link on Pinterest, or make a review of the product on YouTube. You can also write out everything about the product and give it to bloggers to sell. Every time you use a different site, you will be able to further the ability to get the product for other customers to see. The more the product is online for people to see, the more customers will view the product and buy it.

Sixth, think about the shipping cost for each item. While shipping may seem like a small part of selling a product, it does have the ability to become a large concern. If you are selling an average of three items a day and then you jump to selling forty items every day, then you would have to get more supplies for the packaging and spend more time labeling the product for each customer. This is the reason why many sellers will choose to sell their product on Amazon. Being a part of Amazon FBA means that they will handle the shipping of the products. Sellers choose this since Amazon will handle the entire shipping process (including the customer service and returns), the orders can be packed and shipped any day and anytime, and as a seller you have the choice to include free shipping on the items you want to sell. You would not need to hire any staff to help out with the shipping, and Amazon FBA is able to adjust itself to the continual growth of each business.

Finally, remember to sell the product on multiple sites. Amazon is a very popular place to sell products, but there are still other sites to be seen out there online. There are still advantages to selling on eBay, Etsy, and on your own ecommerce website. The more you expose your product online, the more you will see potential customers. The more your product is viewed on these different sites, the more sales you will receive in return. On the other side, you have to be sure that you have enough inventory to handle selling the product on multiple sites. This requires a certain amount of capital and the funds to advance the business. This alone will increase the inventory base so that you can sell to other customers.

With these different techniques, it will be easier to find yourself in the same positions on the common Amazon sellers that known how to work through the system. While there are many techniques above that you can use, there are still more to be found online. Sometimes to give more of a lift to the product, it is best to consider what some of the more successful sellers on Amazon are able to do. The following are some of the strategies used by these sellers.

The first thing these best sellers look to do is taking over the 'buy box.' When a person looks to purchase an item, other sellers might have that same item to sell. The best sellers show on the front page under the 'add to cart' section on the right side. There are normally three of these best sellers that advertise the product for a different or even a lower price. A crucial part of successfully selling on Amazon is winning a spot in this 'buy box'. There are three ways to get that position. The first thing is the pricing of the product. Amazon will automatically find the top three lowest prices for the other sellers. This lowest price must include both the actual price and the shipping of the product. The second thing to do is look at the shipping performance of the product. Amazon has a very large priority on fast and hassle free shipping for the customers. This is why they encourage all of their sellers to be part of the Amazon FBA program. This way all the products could have the fastest shipping so that Amazon would continue getting their high reviews. The shipping performance overall on a product includes multiple variables: the order defect rate and the perfect order percentage. The order defect rate is the number of orders that were canceled, given a negative review, shipped improperly, or returned. The perfect order percentage is the amount of orders that run smoothly without any kind of customer intervention. Amazon is able to keep track of how often a product runs out of supplies, so it is best to make sure that you are able to maintain a complete stock for your own product. The third thing to look at to be a part of the 'buy box' is the seller rating. It is best to have a high rating around ninety percent for the product. Every top seller has at least a rating of ninety percent when they are seen on the front page with the product. Getting a positive feedback about your product and gaining popularity for the item is the best thing to look at for selling. Now that these three tactics have been revealed, the next step is to win over the 'buy box.'

There are two main steps to follow in order to win over the 'buy box.' First, be sure that as a seller you are still eligible in the company. Your product needs to have the same ASIN (step two mentioned below) as the listed you wish to be featured upon. You must also have many reviews on the products to win the spot. Second, lower the price of the product. If you are eligible, then pricing is the only other variable to be concerned about. All that you need to do for this is to find out how much the competitors are selling the product for. See the price, and offer to sell and ship your product for one penny less than them. That one penny will rank you higher and get you a position in the 'buy box.' Either that or you can simply continue to enjoy the benefits of being part of the Amazon FBA program. Being a part of this means that you will receive a special orange FBA icon on the seller listing. You will also to be able to compete against other Amazon prime listings that are available (this reason alone is a good reason to join Amazon FBA). It is important to remember that lower the price will get you a higher rank, but it may not be the best option to maintain when looking at a long-term business strategy. You do not want to compete on price alone when your product is against another.

The second thing that the successful sellers at Amazon do is that they use ASIN piggybacking. When a seller is able to begin their product statement by identifying their product ASIN, they are able to see all the details associated with the product. This ASIN is listed under the Product Details section of the individual product listing. Next, they would need to research the specific manufacturer to make sure that they are able to resell the product by themselves. It is good to be sure that you are able to ship and sell the product on your own to be sure that you get the most amount of sales and profit. Find out how much it would cost for the entire sale and how much it would cost to ship the item. Is there a number between the number you got and one cent that could be less than the current 'buy box' winning price? If there is, then you are able to make an easy profit. If there is not, then you might still be able to work out a deal with the manufacturer if you ask. But, if you do not think that it is worth the time to contact the manufacturer or ship the product on your own, then start to look for other products in the same subject area. The chances are that there is money to be made in a lower ranked product.

There is another term that goes along with ASIN piggybacking, and that is the term Black hat ASIN piggybacking.

Since some of the sellers have been able to develop a black hat form of this piggybacking, they were able to find another way through the system. Basically, a person is able to kick off on other popular products and then they are able to list them with the same ASIN as their other non-knockoff counterparts. This is able to work since it involves the process of Amazon identifying and then spending misleading sellers to other areas. The seller who had a listing that was illegitimately piggybacked would have to order from one of the other suspected counterfeit seller's products in order to prove that it is a different product. It should be said that Amazon does not have anything against selling a cheap knockoff brand of a product. They do not want sellers to lie about what the product is or who made the product. Things happen when selling many products, and some days the wrong product might be chosen since it was taken from the wrong seller. To make sure that this does not happen to you as a seller, make sure that the ASIN piggybacking is above the table. This means that you should make sure that you are shipping the exact same product with the exact same brand and the exact same manufacturing code.

The third thing these successful sellers do is that they hold themselves to custom URL queries. Amazon is able to keep track of the products the people end up buying after they search for a given keyword. They then use the keyword data to decide which products are most relevant to the original search term. This means that you would be able to drive the traffic page using a custom URL to make Amazon see that all of those people used the same keyword and that they came from the same search result. This way, every sale you make a profit from will have a special link associated with the search term. Remember that this is not meant to be a first case scenario. It sometimes works when other times it causes a lower ranking through the Amazon algorithm. The absolute worst case scenario is that you would be getting extra sales to your product. Amazon is not the same as Google where they would punish the seller for trying to optimize the search engine. Since Google runs deeply with search engines, they will punish any seller that attempts to change the URL search keywords.

If you have lots of capital, then you can keep a fast track for yourself with Amazon. Start by searching for a term that you want to be associated with the rank of the product. Click on the product, and then buy it yourself. Change the IP on your own computer or move to a different computer. Do the same thing again with your own same product you are looking to have a higher rating for. Of course, with a high amount of capital comes the same option of using more of the Amazon Product Ads.

The fourth thing that these successful sellers at Amazon look at is the Vender powered coupons. If you are an individual seller with a pro merchant account, or a professional seller, or even a vendor, then you are eligible to use the Amazon built-in promotional tools. The best shoppers at Amazon and the people looking to get the best deal always make use of the Amazon daily deals. You can access these deals by yourself in the 'today's deals' link on the top-most navigation menu that is next to the Amazon logo on the website. This section of the website is an individual department upon itself. The promotions on the product are given their own unique links and their own listing pages. The interesting part to look at on this web page is the coupons link. This page will take you to a list of Amazon's most popular vendor powered coupons in a multitude of categories. There are coupons for outdoor gear, clothing, grocery, household supplies, electronics, personal care, kitchen, science gear, and more. There are coupons for just about everything that is available with one exception, digital content.

With these vender-powered coupons, you will be able to promote any other kinds of Amazon product listing. The coupon pages are able to have their own kind of independent sales rank. If you are a new seller or if you are trying to compete in a tough niche, these coupons will be able to promote your product more than the original listing itself. You will also be able to create a larger discount for yourself than the competition. This is a similar tactic to winning the 'buy box'. Amazon continues to try and five customers the best deal possible. You would only need to be a little bit better than the competition in order to maximize your chances of appearing on the coupons page. You can also promote the party's vendor powered coupons on other third party deal sites. Simply search in Google 'submit a deal' and you will have a large listing of websites that will want to showcase the deal. Submit your coupon to ten of these different sites each day. If your coupon is good enough for buyers to see, then you will start to see the steady flow of consumers coming to buy your product. You can also choose to give out these vender-powered coupons to other friends and family in exchange for reviews. This is where most sellers and clients will have the most amount of success. They will be able to see that the coupons work while trusting the people close to them to give the product a high rating. Having them buy the product through Amazon will help to give more states of reviews for people in Amazon to see. Not everyone is able to make use of these vendor powered coupons or the other promotional tools, but if you have the right kind of account, then it would be good to check out since they can help to maximize products.

The fifth thing that the successful sellers at Amazon do is that they use automated tools. There is a tool called the 'KTD Amazon Keyword Tool' that works with the keyword entry system. When you enter a keyword into the system, then it is able to automatically query with the Amazon search box for the long tail search suggestions. If you are looking for more of a premium alternative, then you can use a program called 'MarchantWords'. This is a system that pulls data from the major search engines and identifies other matching queries in Amazon. Then they are able to use an algorithm to combine the entire set of data and give an estimated traffic of numbers. While these programs do exist and some successful sellers use them, it is not the most recommended choice to use since it does involve going through the programs of Amazon. Besides, the advertising that Amazon FBA provides just for you being a member will bring more worth in income that these programs will.

One program that is very good to have to keep track of management in products is called 'InventoryLab'. This program or software is an all in one inventory management system. Here, you would be able to create your own product listing and keep track of the shipments, inventory, income, and expenses. You would be able to analyze the business's growth and performance over a long period of time. However, this type of program is recommended if you are only selling products on Amazon. If you selling products on Amazon and other sites, then the program 'SellBrite' might work better for you. This is a program that would be able to sacrifice the accounting, financial tools, and analytical tools found in InventoryLab. Instead, these tools are replaced with a multi-channel inventory and listing of management tools.

Being able to sell on Amazon should not be a big hassle to your daily routine and doesn't have to be intimidating. Even as the seller, it is still a great place to sell products with and maintain a connection with. They are one of the largest ecommerce platforms in the world, and so far, you have read through many different strategies for how to get through it in the most successful way possible. They are able to help you along the way and they are able to provide a stable platform for your business to rely upon.

CHAPTER EIGHT

GETTING REVIEWS

When getting feedback from buyers, the most important thing to remember is that it is the buyer's choice to leave a review. Even if you ask them to leave a review, they still have a choice to say if they liked the product or not. Do not be discouraged if you do not have much feedback. It takes time and patience to wait for more customers. As more people buy the product, there will be more people who will most likely be willing to leave a review. Once one person leaves a review, then more people will begin to follow the chain on giving feedback.

The next step to follow is attempting to keep a high feedback rating for the products. In order to keep a higher feedback rating, the first thing to look at is the condition of the product. When you need to state the condition of the product, try to round down instead of up. For example, if you are selling a hardcover book that is somewhere between a 'very good' and a 'good' condition, say that it is in a 'good' condition. The person who buys this book will see that they got a better deal since it was given a smaller label for the review. Buyers themselves can be rather picky about the stated condition of the product and the actual condition of the product. If they think they are ordering a book in an 'excellent' condition but they receive it in a 'good' condition, then they will not be pleased. They will not feel that they received a great deal from you. Once this happens, some buyers will give a negative form of feedback on the product because the condition they received the product in was lower than the stated condition. Since people grade items and products differently, it is best to be safe in order to receive a positive rating.

Secondly, you should think twice about selling a product in a low condition. A low condition on Amazon is labeled as 'acceptable' which is not the easiest way to sell a product. What one person might see as acceptable, another might see as disgraceful. Even if you are able to provide the buyer with a detailed condition mentioning every detailed note about the product, they still may not agree with the condition of the item. Let's say they read the description and they decide to buy the product, but then they forget about what they read about the product when they receive it. Once they receive the product, they might leave a negative review since it is in a lower condition. Yes, you explained the condition completely, but that may not have been enough to save yourself from a negative review. This is why it is best to not sell items that are not the greatest in quality.

The third thing to look at is how quickly you should act when you receive negative feedback. Most of the time, these cases of negative feedback are going to come from the price of the product. It is against Amazon's policy for a buyer to leave feedback for a specific seller if that feedback is related to another product review or another price. As soon as you receive negative feedback from a buyer, see if they were fair or unfair in the review. If they were unfair, then open up a ticket with seller support. Talk to them and ask them to remove the feedback since it goes against the feedback guidelines.

Whenever you describe your own reasons of feedback to Amazon, remember to limit the number of words you use. The longer the explanation is, the more likely it will be ignored by the seller support staff. They could potentially ignore the bulk of the message and completely deny the feedback removal request. When you are communicating or writing to Amazon, it is best to be concise and get straight to the point. Most of the time, the seller support staff will understand your perspective and will remove the unfair negative feedback. If they choose to deny your request, then the goal of feedback removal continues. The next step to removing the feedback is to write out another ticket to the seller support and then hope that the next Amazon staff member will read and understand your reasoning to remove the feedback.

The fourth task to consider is acting quickly, apologetically, and generously to the legitimate negative feedback. It is possible that the book you sold was covered in highlights and you forgot to mention that detail. The consumer would leave a completely fair negative feedback. It is possible that you sold a used music CD that you did not test before selling it, so the consumer sees that the CD skips every other song track. This is another case where it is completely understandable, and the buyer is reasonable for leaving a negative review. When the seller support cannot remove the feedback for you, the buyer can. The moment you receive fair negative feedback about your product, send a friendly email to the buyer. Explain to them that you were mistaken and that you are sorry for any inconvenience. Communicating with the buyer in order to notify them that you were wrong and that you understand the error will show a kind of responsibility on your side as well as showing appreciation for what went wrong. Ask the buyer if there is anything that you can do to make up for the error made in the product. Mention how important customer satisfaction is to you and that you want to do anything you can to make it up to them. It is sometimes best to even offer a gift card to Amazon. But do not ask then to remove the feedback in this email, as that email comes later.

Once the buyer has seen the email and accepted the apology, it is now time to send out another email to say once again how important customer satisfaction is to you. Send this email a few days later with the gift card and then ask them again if there is anything you can do for them. Remind them that your feedback score is very important to you since you are a small seller on Amazon. Most people are quite supportive of small businesses and they may feel empathy for you. Ask them politely if they would be able to remove the feedback only if they feel as if you have made up for the error. Give them a link or provide them with instructions on how to remove the negative feedback. Most of the time, a satisfied customer will understand your position and be willing to remove the feedback. Do not connect the idea of the gift card to the removal of the negative feedback. Do not mention both of these things in the same sentence. It is against Amazon's policy to offer a gift card in exchange for removing a form of negative feedback. Not having them in the same sentence will be a safer way of communicating the message through in order to be sure that you do not receive a penalty from Amazon and that you do not make a wrong message to the buyer.

The fifth thing to do is use Feedback Genius. This is a program that will help to not only stop the negative feedback, but it will help to increase the amount of positive feedback you receive. This program easily connects itself to your Amazon account and will work to automatically send the customer an email to let them know that the order has been delivered. They are able to do this by looking at the tracking number and package information. Feedback Genius is then able to ask the customer if they were satisfied with their order and it will ask them to leave a review on Amazon for you. They will also inform the customer that if they had any kind of negative issue with the product that they should contact you directly about the problem first so that you can address and solve the issue quickly. This nips in the bud the possibility of negative feedback by giving you an option to make the customer happy before they even get a chance to leave a negative review.

A few days after the customer receives the package, if they have not left a review on the product, then Feedback Genius will send them another email to remind them to leave a positive review or to contact you if they experienced any kind of problem. Most of the time, feedback scores double with the use of this program. One of the most popular features of this program is the text updates. Once you receive feedback with a score of three or lower, they will send you a text that you have gotten negative feedback. Once this happens, you can act on the negative feedback quickly by using the strategies discussed above. The delays in waiting to check email can be either hours or days depending on how much you are around the computer. If you receive negative feedback and do not know about it for five hours, then during that five hours you could be losing sales since other customers would see the negative comment and think that the product is not worth buying.

When signing up for Feedback Genius for the first time, one of the best parts about it is that you can try it for free. You do not have to enter a credit card number, you will have it for a full sixty days, and you will be able to receive five hundred free messages. Giving this program a try with that much to offer is a great deal to have. Simply seeing how much it helps to remind people to give positive reviews is another reason why this would be a good program to have on your side.

Increasing Product Reviews

As a seller on Amazon, it is best to aim for many product reviews in order to give people a widespread opinion on how good your product is. Once a seller has begun to do this and successfully create a solid foundation for themselves with reviews, then they will be able to transition themselves to a deeper campaign for the product. Sellers should aim to base their strategy off of other keywords and research for the business to see what kind of reviews and how many reviews they are competing against.

While reviews are not the only component that sellers should look to base their review off of, they do help the seller to see what other people think of the product. They should try and aim for a higher level of competition in the market in order to stand out. For example, if the first page of items has about three hundred reviews, they the sellers for the competing items should try to gain that many reviews or even succeed that amount of reviews. Sellers should focus more on the amount of reviews they have rather than the amount of inventory they have. While it is important to maintain a balance in the life of a business, it is also important to keep up with the buyers of the product and remember that they control the amount of income you receive. If people are continually saying that they do not enjoy the product, then you will have a rather low amount of sales.

To get reviews quickly for the first product you are selling on Amazon, try to reach out to family and friends for help. These are people you have learned to trust and you can trust them to leave a review for you when getting started. Another way to get reviews is by reaching out to bloggers. They will see your product and they work to spread news quickly among their own followers and groups of people. After giving your product link to bloggers, go onto Facebook and give out coupons for your product. Giving the product away for half off will get more people to buy it since they will have more control over getting a deal with the coupon code. These few things can help to raise the amount of reviews you receive for the product. In return, this will raise the amount of popularity you get on the item and it will give your product a higher ranking in Amazon.

Another way to get reviews from people is with email follow up campaigns. While these are sometimes not the greatest way to get the most amount of reviews possible, they will be able to communicate the product through the traffic of customers. This will give people the chance to review the product and then they will also want to leave more of a positive review since they saw everything your product was worth. There are other email campaigns that involve being a part of the customer's influence on your ranking. These were mentioned above with removing negative feedback. This is where you send emails to the customer to apologize for any kind of inconvenience and you offer then another product to make them pleased with your way of selling items.

One of the new review services that may help for you to use is called Review Kick. Being able to have reviews is the product listing will help by itself to have more reviews generated naturally from people. This is a different type of program where you as a seller can make a deal with the buyer. If they agree to leave an honest review for you, then they can have a large discount when buying the product. It is completely free to list the product, and it is also free to request the product as a reviewer (a person who reviews products naturally and posts them on YouTube and other social media sites).

There are a few things that makes Review Kick different from the other sites. This is a unique service where the seller is able to approve all the different reviewers. All of the reviewers who have requested the product must also be able to share their own Amazon reviewer profile. This is to ensure that the people you are communicating with are able to see that they are honest with leaving a review for you as the seller. Also, you have the control to approve every code that is sent out for reviewing. One of the perks of this program is that it is a free program to have. There are other reviews sites out there that will charge sellers in multiple different ways. This program is completely free for both buyers and sellers. The next great thing to know about this program is how all of the reviewers must leave a review. It is understandable that every discount given out by the seller has a cost to it. Because of this, the program wants to be sure that the launch and reviewer promotions are as cost effective as possible. Whenever someone requests a code, they will be forced to follow the community guidelines of the Review Kick program, and then they must be able to leave an honest Amazon review. The final thing to remember about this program is how it is all within Amazon's guidelines.

One of the best ways to get reviews is through customer experience. Many negative reviews about a product can be misled. You have to remember to be honest about what you are selling. Provide as much detailed information as possible that is precise and accurate information about the product. It is also important to complete the customer experience by sending follow up emails after the buyer has purchased the product. Mention in the email how thankful you were for them choosing your product out of all the other products available to them, and ask for them to leave a review on your product. This should be more of a generic email rather than something special.

The last thing to do to get more reviews for your product is looking at the reviews from the top Amazon reviewers. Being able to look at what they are doing and writing to them may help for you to create a connection for your product to grow from. These are the people that know how to get through to the buyers of Amazon and they know how to grow on a strong foundation. They know how to get through with a large portion of products, and they know how to find their own balance in finding more sales for their own product. The top reviews can be found through a simple search for the top ten Amazon reviewers on Google. Reaching out to them through email will be able to give you more advice on how to get started with reviews on Amazon and what they did to have the higher connections in the company.

Remember to thank them in the email for their time and thoughtful advice. It is important to maintain a positive image of yourself to another who is connected to your own product on Amazon.

Optimizing Your Listing

Being able to optimize your listing in the right way will help you to stand out in competition against the other products. While you are selling products on Amazon, it is important to remember that you are in a business that is selling brand name products under the name Amazon. You are continually looking to have more reviews, higher review ratings, a higher rating on your product, more income from sales, and a chance to be part of the 'buy box' section on the front page. If you have read through and become part of the ecommerce section of websites, then you already know how much the impact of ideas can influence a business.

The first part of optimizing the listing is to take the first step of getting the listing out on the market. Uploading the listing onto Amazon is done through CSV files in the seller central inventory. Here you will be able to find a tool to show the right category for the product and you will be able to add the file that you need to download. Fill out the information and then upload the file again in order to get the product on the marketplace. While this file and way of getting your product online may look overwhelming at first, it is overall simple to use. There are lots of questions to fill out and there are lots of instructions that you are able to follow in order to get to the market quickly. If you need to add another product later on, then you can either use this method again or you can go to the inventory section and edit the inventory to add the new product.

The next part of optimizing your listing is to give your product title a good first impression. Some of the basic principles and fundamental ideas follow the title of the product. The title of the listing is the most important place to target the product's audience through the use of certain keywords and information. You will want to use the title to bring your customers to your product, attract them to the sale, and inform them about the quality of the product. You do not want to confuse the customers will lots of random keywords strung together into one massive title. Instead, you should follow these next few things and be sure that these things are in your title. The first thing to have is a brand name. Amazon themselves will recommend this as the first case of action for almost every product. The top sellers at Amazon will prove that you do not always need to have brand name listed, but it does help to have as a basic keyword for the product. The second thing to have is keywords. These are used in order to give a description to your product and allow the customer to know what the product does. The title should include keywords that are normally searched for. The Amazon search engine will not recognize commas, so it is best to separate the keywords with a space. You will want to try and have at least three different keyword phrases as a basic target for your product. The third thing to have is the right terms for the color, quantity, variation, and model number of the product. If you are selling an item in bulk, then the number or items in the product is important to specify. If you are selling an item of a certain color, then it is important to specify that certain color. Put these kind of details in the title, but closer to the end of it. Electronics will need to have the model number included so that the buyers are able to compare the products of the same model number. It is important to notice that Amazon has limited their amount of words they are allowing in the title. They are not going to allow sellers to have their product with a title of over two hundred characters. This is to ensure that people will not stuff their product titles with tons of keywords and overcrowd the website. If your product goes over the limit, it simply will not exist on the site. They will not allow the product to be viewed until you have gone through and fixed the length of the title. Overall, it is important for the title to be clear and easy to read in order to draw in more customers each and every day.

Inside of each product detail there are hidden search terms and keywords that are valued for finding each product. The search terms have a high value on what buyers are able to see on the whole list of products on Amazon. It is very similar in the same way that Google uses search terms to narrow down the information to give people what they are searching for. On Amazon, you will be able to put in one to five different search terms or keywords depending on the category. The target audience keywords for a product are more specific for each product. If you are selling dresses, then one of your keywords to write in would be 'women'. Platinum keywords are some of the few selected keywords that allow your advertising in the product to have more browsing locations. Most people do not use these since they are not the most important words to be focused on for the product.

In the listing of your product, remember that bullet points should be used not only to organize the information, but it is easier for the buyer to view the information of the product in these bullet points. The bullet points will draw more attention to the product and will give more of an opportunity to highlight and draw out the important points of the product for the customer to quickly read through in a neat format and style. Every seller gets to use five bullet points, and these five bullet points are the best way to re-touch upon the keywords and information in the title. Almost every seller does a great job using these points by optimizing these keywords within each bullet point. Amazon will even recommend the seller to use these bullet points in order to gain more sales on the product. The bullet point suggestions will be able to help describe the product quickly and give more keywords for your product to follow.

The last thing to look at for the product page is the photos attached to the description. Amazon will allow each product to have up to seven photos with their item. They must be within a certain resolution range in order to use the zoom feature. This is helpful for buyers to see different parts of the product at a closer view. They can then see more detail of a different section and choose if that is the product they want to have. Since many products have multiple different components, it is helpful to see what the product has as a part of it. On smartphones, they are beginning to have the matching resolutions on the website, but it is still important to follow through with the regulations of the image size and resolution.

All of these factors can be used to optimize your own product listing. It is important to follow different strategies in order to find the right balance of selling and getting reviews from people. While there are many strategies listed in these chapters, there are more to find online if you need more paths to follow or if you need to follow a different way to sell the product on Amazon. Either way, there are many benefits to be a part of Amazon FBA, and they themselves can help you to have the most amount of success in selling your product.

CONCLUSION

I hope you have gleaned valuable information from this book, and you will use it to your advantage. Amazon's FBA is a great structure in which to set up your sales business. You should never stop researching and certainly should look at the official sources from Amazon, Alibaba, and any other site you will be using. Once you start making profits you want to know how much money is going where. If fees are too high in one area, optimize such that they fall.

Whether you are a major brand already or just starting out, FBA can benefit you. If you already have a website and inventory management system, you do not need to ditch it to work with FBA. If you don't have those, you can rest assured that Amazon has resources to help you. Furthermore, Amazon offers a plethora of services to assist the operations of your business. From packaging and labeling to customer service and nationwide distribution, you can choose the best set up for yourself and your business.

Once you set up your strategy with Amazon, you will need to find suppliers. There are hundreds of firms out there that want to make money and will help you in the process. If you are selling a product that is ideal for FBA, you will likely find suppliers in China. This is not the only place to find suppliers, but it is rather likely if your product is light, cheap, and easily reproducible. If you are your own supplier, though, Amazon can still help you with the logistics of distribution and warehousing.

After you get your business established and generating profits, you may eventually decide you want to exit. There are numerous ways to exit, and you won't have to choose any at the outset. However, it is good to know the ways you can leave in the future to ensure peace of mind. Knowing which parts you may want to delegate to someone else, or setting a goal for yourself at which point you are willing to walk away, will give your mind a deadline to strive for, releasing any guilt from walking away.

Overall, FBA is a great service that can help your business grow – or even to start. You will get access to Amazon's state-of-the-art robotics and logistics networks as well as their discounted pricing schemes with preferred carriers. You don't need to look far to see that the world is going online. Amazon is not the only website that offers retail services to customers, and I urge you to do more research. But it is a great place to start if you need to take your business online or if you need a reputable, well-run company to take over the logistics part of your business.

I wish you the best of luck in your endeavors and happy money-making.